I0827735

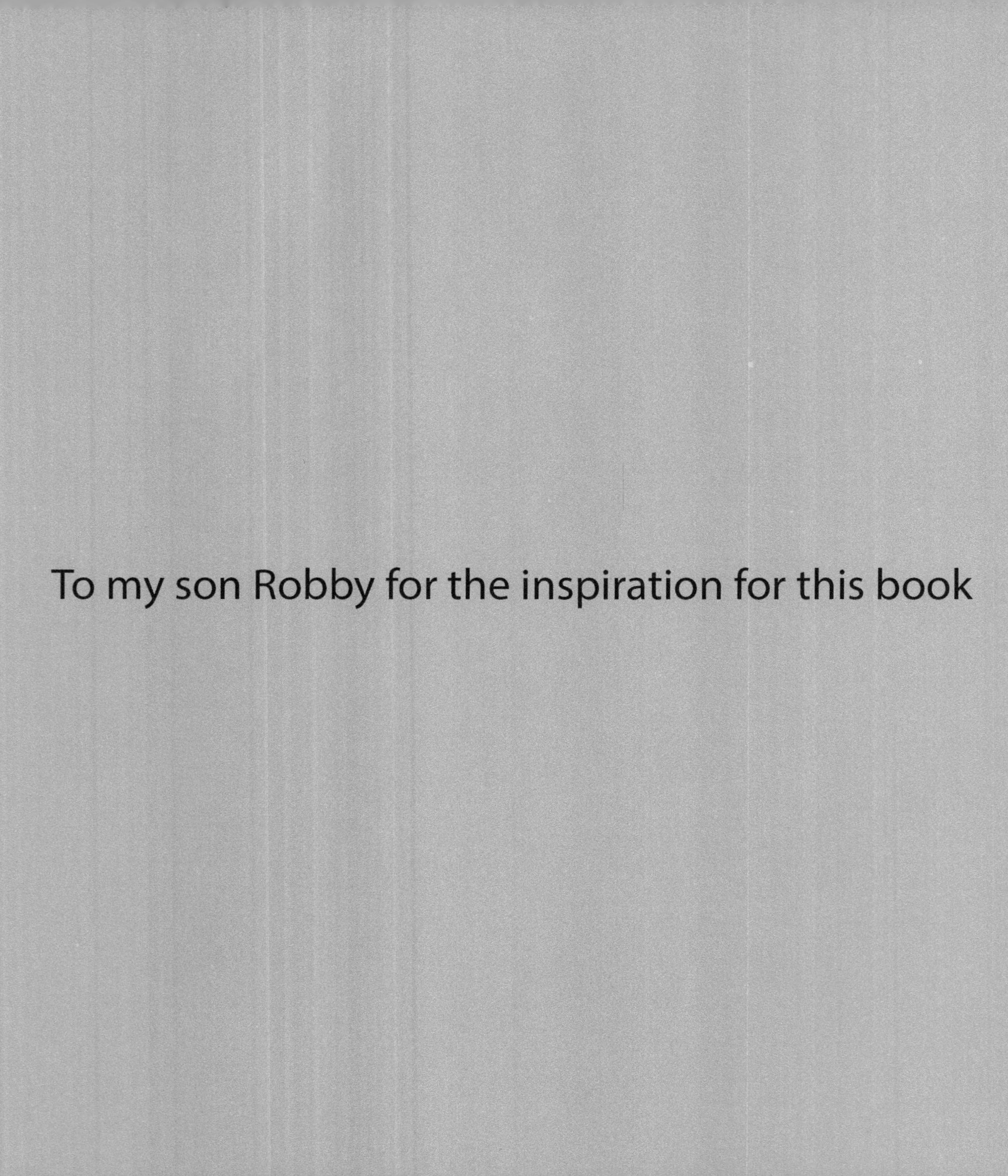

To my son Robby for the inspiration for this book

Daddy loves you when you are sick.

Daddy loves you if you would rather play with babies or tea, than play football outside with daddy.

Daddy loves you if you like puppies and not snakes.

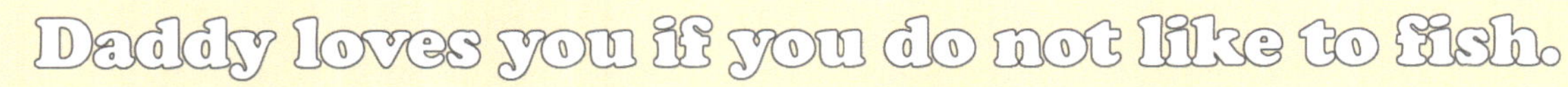
Daddy loves you if you do not like to fish.

Daddy loves you if you do not like to camp.

Daddy loves you when you fall down and get hurt.

Daddy loves you when you do not clean your room.

Daddy loves you when you do not eat all your dinner.

Daddy loves you if you let him play with you.

Daddy loves you if you want to play with someone else

Daddy loves you if you dress yourself

Daddy loves you if you
do your hair yourself.

Daddy loves you if you do daddy's hair for him

Daddy loves you when you are not supposed
to be jumping on the bed

Daddy loves you when you are asleep.

Daddy loves you if you are mad at him for putting you in time out for not listening

Daddy loves you if you play in the rain.

Daddy loves you if you play in the mud,
and get all muddy from head to toe

Daddy loves you when you are with him

Daddy loves you if you are with someone else

Daddy loves you no matter what.

Just like God loves all of us.
No matter what.